TEEN STRONG

Fighting Climate Change WITH

Greta Thunberg

by Kristy Stark

FAST READS

full tilt
PRESS

Greta Thunberg
TEEN STRONG

Full Tilt Press
42964 Osgood Road
Fremont, CA 94539
readfulltilt.com

Full Tilt Press publications may be purchased for educational, business, or sales promotional use.

Editorial Credits
Design and layout by Sara Radka
Edited by Renae Gilles
Copyedited by Nikki Ramsay

Image Credits
Getty Images: DigitalVision Vectors/beastfromeast, background, DisobeyArt, cover (accent), E+/
fotoVoyager, 9, Epsilon/Oleg Nikishin, 7, EyeEm/Khatawut Chaemchamras, 29 (top), EyeEm/
Wathanyu Kanthawong, 29 (bottom), Maja Hitij, 6, 10, Minas Panagiotakis, 24, Moment/twomeows,
21, Sarah Silbiger, 12, Sean Gallup, 15, Spencer Platt, 4, 20, Stephanie Keith, 16, 18, 27 (bottom),
Town & Country/Bryan Bedder, 25 (bottom), WIRED/Matt Winkelmeyer, 25 (top), WPA Pool/
Kirsty Wigglesworth, 27 (top); Newscom: Pacific Press/Michael Nigro, 22, SIPA/AGF/Nicola Marfisi,
19, Polaris, 23, ZUMA Press/NurPhoto/Beata Zawrzel, 8; Pixabay: Free-Photos, 25 (middle);
Shutterstock: trgrowth, 17, Anders Hellberg, cover (main), 1, 3, 11, 14, 26, ProtoplasmaKid, 26

ISBN: 978-1-62920-840-4 (library binding)
ISBN: 978-1-62920-852-7 (ePub)

CONTENTS

SKOLSTREJK
FÖR
KLIMATET

Introduction

On August 28, 2019, 16-year-old Greta Thunberg stood on the deck of a yacht. It sailed past the Statue of Liberty in New York City. People on other boats welcomed Greta. They held signs with messages about how to help the planet.

Large crowds stood on the dock. People cheered, and Greta waved to them. Reporters waited for her to make a statement. Her message about **climate change** and protecting the planet was clear. "Let's not wait any longer. Let's do it now."

It had taken two weeks to sail from the United Kingdom to New York City. Greta made the trip to attend a meeting on climate change at the **United Nations** (UN). She spoke to the UN on September 23, 2019.

People may wonder why she did not fly on a plane, which would have taken hours instead of days. Those people have a lot to learn about this outspoken teenager and what she stands for.

climate change: abnormal change in Earth's climate patterns caused by fossil fuels

United Nations: an organization formed in 1945 so that its member countries could work together and cooperate better

Getting Started

Greta has said Rosa Parks is one of her greatest inspirations. Parks was a leader of the nonviolent civil rights movement (1950s–1960s), which fought for equal rights for African Americans in the United States.

reta Ernman Thunberg was born on January 3, 2003. She was born in Stockholm, Sweden. Her mom is an opera singer named Malena Ernman. Ernman is well known in Sweden. Greta's dad is Svante Thunberg. He is an actor and author. Beata is Greta's younger sister.

At age 11, a doctor said that Greta had Asperger's syndrome. It is a type of **autism spectrum disorder** (ASD). Many people with it have strong verbal skills and are very smart. Many are able to focus intensely on a task until it is complete. They often have a strong attention to detail too. But some may have problems with being social and talking to others.

Greta has had these strengths and challenges her whole life. She has felt "invisible" because she is shy. It is not easy for her to talk with people.

Growing up with a famous singer for a mother has helped prepare Greta for her own fame.

As of 2018, 1 in every 38 boys has been diagnosed with ASD in the United States. The rate for girls is 1 in 152.

autism spectrum disorder: a disorder where someone may have difficulties in social interaction and communication, and in restricted or repetitive patterns of thought and behavior

At age 15, Greta spoke at the 24th Conference of the Parties to the UN Framework Convention on Climate Change. During the conference, she said, "I've learned you are never too small to make a difference."

Learning about Climate Change

Greta's ASD has helped spark her mission too. Greta first learned about climate change through a documentary she watched. She was just eight years old. This knowledge changed her life. The girl was outraged when she learned the effects of **fossil fuels**. She did not know why more people were not mad too. Greta wanted to learn more about it. She read articles and watched films about climate change.

Greta could not stop thinking about this global crisis. It made her very sad for a few months. Her parents were worried about her. Their daughter finally told them what was bothering her.

The conversation sparked changes in her home. Greta had learned that planes have the highest **emissions**. Her mom flew in planes for her job. The girl convinced her mom to give up flying. Greta also learned about the **carbon footprint** from animal products. She became vegan, giving up all animal products, while her dad gave up eating meat.

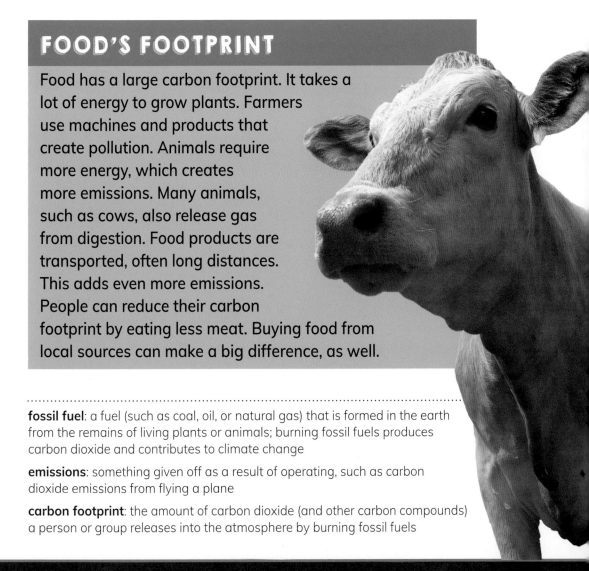

FOOD'S FOOTPRINT

Food has a large carbon footprint. It takes a lot of energy to grow plants. Farmers use machines and products that create pollution. Animals require more energy, which creates more emissions. Many animals, such as cows, also release gas from digestion. Food products are transported, often long distances. This adds even more emissions. People can reduce their carbon footprint by eating less meat. Buying food from local sources can make a big difference, as well.

fossil fuel: a fuel (such as coal, oil, or natural gas) that is formed in the earth from the remains of living plants or animals; burning fossil fuels produces carbon dioxide and contributes to climate change

emissions: something given off as a result of operating, such as carbon dioxide emissions from flying a plane

carbon footprint: the amount of carbon dioxide (and other carbon compounds) a person or group releases into the atmosphere by burning fossil fuels

Becoming Teen Strong

Greta does not like being the center of attention. "I have to tell myself it's for a good cause. I am trying to say something with all this attention, to use my platform to do something good," she said.

SKOLSTREJK
FÖR
TET

Greta helped make changes in her family. She wanted to make changes in the world around her too. This desire led to a bold move. On Monday, August 20, 2018, she started to sit outside the Swedish **Parliament**. The teen was determined to protest until the general election on September 9, 2018. She skipped school for three weeks. Each day, she held a sign that said, "School **strike** for climate." Greta hoped to force leaders to take steps to reduce climate change.

Greta's sign translates to "school strike for climate."

In 2016, 55 countries had signed the UN's Paris Agreement. As of 2019, 185 countries had signed it. This document has goals to help fight climate change. It states ways to cut pollution. It requires countries to report their emissions. This is the first global effort to deal with climate change.

Sweden signed the agreement. But Greta felt that leaders were not trying to follow the plan. It seemed to her that they cared more about being popular than helping the planet. So Greta began her school strike.

Greta got the idea to stage a school strike from other students. Those teens were survivors of a school shooting in Parkland, Florida.

parliament: a group of people responsible for making laws in certain kinds of governments, or the building where those people work

strike: when someone stops working or going to school in order to force someone else to agree to do something

While school strikes are not very common in the United States, they are popular in Europe.

A Growing Movement

From the start, Greta used social media to spread her ideas. A picture of her serious face and her strike sign summed up her message for Instagram users. After a few weeks, she protested only on Fridays. She started to call the school strikes "Fridays for Future."

No one joined Greta when she first started to protest. Some people ignored her as they walked by. Others made fun of her and said mean things. She was on her own. But that soon started to change. Classmates and teachers joined her within weeks.

People around the world took notice too. By November 2018, the Friday climate strikes became a global event for at least 17,000 students in 24 countries. By March 2019, there were people in 135 countries striking.

People looked to Greta as the leader of the cause. The quiet girl started to speak out more and more. She was driven by her desire to protect the future of the planet.

GRETA'S INSTAGRAM FOLLOWERS

Greta continues to use social media to speak out. The number of people following her keeps rising at a fast pace. In March 2019, she had about 500,000 Instagram followers. By January 2020, she had more than 9 million followers! More people hear her message about climate change each day.

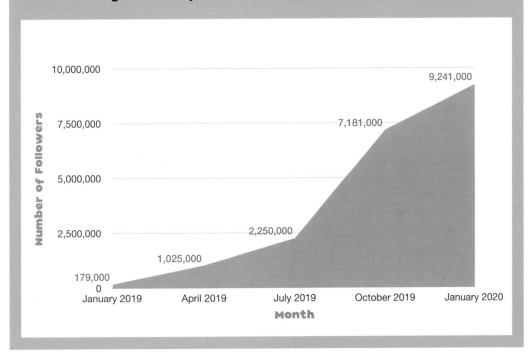

Sparking a Movement

Greta is demanding that citizens and lawmakers take climate change seriously. "I want you to act as you would in a crisis. I want you to act as if the house was on fire. Because it is," she said in a 2019 speech.

Greta works to protect the future of the planet. She calls for world leaders to make new laws. The laws would require countries to find cleaner sources of energy than fossil fuels.

In part, climate change is caused by high levels of **carbon dioxide**. This gas comes from burning fossil fuels. These include coal, oil, and natural gas. They are used for energy to make heat. They help make fuel for cars, boats, and planes too.

Moving away from fossil fuels and toward clean energy is a huge task. Factories, businesses, and the public have to change. Greta insists that people start now.

Greta regularly joins protests around Europe, including a Fridays for Future march in Berlin in 2019.

Close to 65 percent of electricity used in the United States comes from fossil fuels.

carbon dioxide: a colorless, odorless gas that is naturally present in air, but which is also produced by burning fossil fuels, which contributes to climate change

Protests

Greta's protests, speeches, and videos have gone **viral**. She has sparked a global movement of weekly protests. Thousands of people now protest around the world each Friday. They join her in raising awareness about the global climate crisis.

Greta and her supporters all work to put pressure on **lawmakers** to listen to data about how climate change is affecting the planet. Greta believes that if people use this data, they will be compelled to cut the use of fossil fuels.

Greta has said repeatedly that lawmakers need to "listen to the science." Climate change has been difficult for scientists to predict, leading many people to ignore their findings.

So how did a teen start a global movement? She did so by being persistent and focused. Her speeches are straightforward and easy to follow. She speaks with emotion, including anger. Her points are backed up by science.

viral: spread very quickly to many people, usually via the internet

lawmaker: an elected government official who helps create laws that people must follow

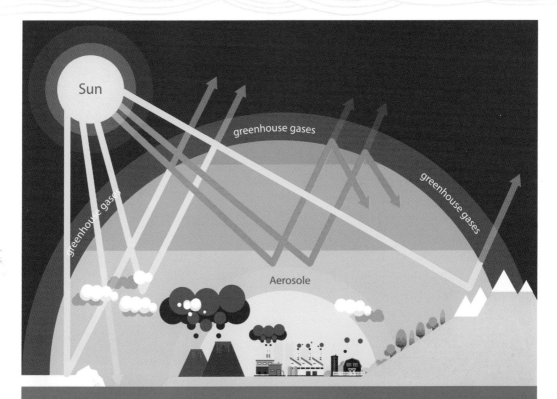

THE GREENHOUSE EFFECT

1. Fossil fuels are burned to make energy to heat homes and fuel vehicles. The process of burning fossil fuels produces carbon dioxide.

2. Carbon dioxide gets trapped in Earth's **atmosphere**.

3. The sun warms the surface of Earth and the air above it. The trapped gases get warmed too. Some of the heat is not able to escape.

4. The warming of trapped gases over time increases the temperature of the atmosphere. This is called the greenhouse effect.

....

atmosphere: the air that surrounds a planet

work in Progress

Greta was part of the first-ever UN Youth Climate Summit in 2019. Youths from more than 140 countries attended.

Greta is not just the face of youth climate change efforts. She's the voice of the movement too. She has given countless speeches to people of all ages. In fact, many of her speeches were put into a book. The book is called *No One Is Too Small to Make a Difference*. It was published in June 2019. Authoring a book was one more way for her to spread her message.

Greta visits many countries to speak and join meetings. She usually travels by train, which creates less pollution per person than cars.

World leaders have turned to Greta too. US congresswoman Alexandria Ocasio-Cortez has praised Greta's efforts and listened to her ideas about what can be done to help this crisis.

Greta believes that the rules have to change to save the planet. The old way of doing things has not helped. So the teenager tells world leaders to listen to the facts. She tells them that people and ecosystems are dying. "We are in the beginning of a mass extinction," Greta said. She works to convince them that immediate action is needed. Although Greta is not a scientist, she challenges everyone to listen to scientists who have studied climate change for many years.

A band called The 1975 teamed up with Greta to record a song. On the track, her voice can be heard reading an essay she'd written. She says, "Everything needs to change. And it has to start today."

Recognition

In March 2019, Greta was nominated for a Nobel Peace Prize. This prize is given to people who have changed the world in peaceful ways. It is a high honor to be considered for the award.

In May 2019, Greta was on the cover of *TIME* magazine. She was named one of the world's most influential people.

Greta's father joined her for her voyage from the United Kingdom to New York.

Later that year, Greta was invited to the UN **summit** in New York. But she worried about how to get there. Flying on a plane was not an option for her. Planes released 895 million tons of carbon dioxide in 2018 alone. This is the exact thing that Greta fights. So she traveled on a zero-emissions boat. It used **renewable energy** instead of fuel. It was one more way to send a message about steps all humans should take to reduce climate change.

THE POWER OF LAWMAKERS

Lawmakers play a huge role in the future of climate change. They can make laws that impact the emissions produced by companies. For example, laws can be made that require factories to be more energy efficient. This can reduce emissions from power plants. New laws could also make sure that tax money is used to update **energy grids**. Then they would work more efficiently. Laws could also require that a certain amount of money goes toward finding ways to use renewable energy sources with less emissions.

summit: a meeting between the leaders of two or more governments

renewable energy: energy that comes from a source that cannot be used up or destroyed, such as wind or solar power

energy grid: a transmission system for electricity; power providers and consumers connected into one network by power lines

A Bright Future

While many people, including politicians and reporters, have criticized Greta, her following continues to grow beyond measure.

In 2019, Greta made plans to pursue activism full time. She took a year off school to do so. In December 2019, she attended the 25th UN Climate Change meeting in Madrid, Spain. Again, she decided to travel there by boat.

That same month, Greta was named *TIME* magazine's Person of the Year. She is the youngest individual to ever receive the title. *TIME* said Greta has turned people's fears about climate change into "a worldwide movement calling for urgent change."

Her location is changing during her year away from school, but her mission is not. Greta will keep up the Friday protests. She is bound to do so until world leaders make big changes. She wants to see efforts made to protect Earth's future.

Strikes and protests are forms of nonviolent resistance. While they draw attention to issues, legal battles are often needed to create change.

Students do not have to go to school for grades 10 through 12 in Sweden. Those grades are optional. That is why Greta can take a year off school.

While in Canada in 2019, Greta led a march and met with politicians. Prime Minister Justin Trudeau said, "I agree with her entirely. We need to do more."

Teen Strong

Greta Thunberg is Teen Strong in both her words and her actions. Time after time, she has stood up for what she believes. She has not backed down to any world leader. Nor does she intend to do so.

Greta's ideas and determination pack a powerful punch. She once gave a speech to the British Parliament. She boldly told the leaders of the country what she thought of their lack of action. She said that their conduct related to the climate crisis "will no doubt be remembered in history as one of the greatest failures of humankind."

Her strength has inspired many people. Perhaps more than any other teen in history, she has stirred a large movement. Millions of young people have called upon world leaders to make changes.

The once invisible girl has commanded the world's attention. A group of fossil fuel companies called her and young activists the "greatest threat" to their business. Greta tweeted her thanks. She said it was the "biggest compliment yet."

YOUNG ACTIVISTS

Vic Barrett is a climate justice activist. Vic and 21 other young people are suing the US government for its role in greenhouse gases. "Climate change isn't just about temperatures and weather, it's about people. Our earth will be here for millennia, it's up to us to decide if humanity will be too," he said.

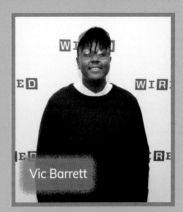

Vic Barrett

Autumn Peltier also spoke at the 2019 climate summit. Autumn is an activist for water conservation and water rights for indigenous peoples. "No child should grow up not knowing what clean water is or never know what running water is," she said in 2018.

In 2019, **Isra Hirsi** turned 16 years old. Like Greta, she takes a stand against climate change. Isra is a co-founder of US Youth Climate Strike. This group seeks to get teens involved in protests around the United States. Isra influences some important people in the **US Congress** too. Her mom is Congresswoman Ilhan Omar from Minnesota. Omar challenges other members of Congress to "listen to the wisdom of our kids!"

Isra Hirsi

US Congress: a group of lawmakers in the US government, made up of the Senate and the House of Representatives

Timeline

January 3, 2003

Greta is born in Stockholm, Sweden. Her parents are Malena Ernman and Svante Thunberg.

2011

At age eight, Greta watches a documentary about climate change. This is the first time she hears of the problem.

August 20, 2018

Greta stages her first school strike outside the Swedish Parliament.

February 2019

Protests inspired by Greta take place in more than 30 countries around the world.

March 2019

Greta is nominated for a Nobel Peace Prize.

July 2019

Lawmakers ask people to boycott Greta's visit to the French Parliament.

August 14, 2019

Greta leaves the United Kingdom on her zero-emissions boat journey to New York City.

September 23, 2019

Greta addresses the UN Climate Change Action Summit. That same day, she and 15 other young people file a complaint with the UN. They argue that five countries have violated their rights by failing to protect children from climate change and its future consequences.

2020

Greta teams up with BBC Studios to create a documentary TV series on the young activist.

QUIZ

#1

How old was Greta when she sailed to New York City?

#2

What percent of US electricity comes from fossil fuels?

#3

How did Greta first learn about climate change?

#4

What did Greta call her Friday school strikes?

#5

What is the name of Greta's book?

#6

What is teen activist Isra Hirsi taking a stand against?

6. Climate change
5. No One Is Too Small to Make a Difference
4. Fridays for Future
3. A documentary
2. 65
1. 16

ACTIVITY

Climate change is a global problem. It threatens the daily lives of citizens around the world. Research another global crisis, including ways to make a difference.

MATERIALS

- computer with internet access
- library access
- pencil and paper

STEPS

1. Choose another crisis that affects most of the world and its citizens.

2. Research to find out what has caused the crisis and how it affects people's daily lives. Also research how the problem can be stopped or helped.

3. Take notes of your findings.

4. Then write a speech to convince your classmates, friends, and family to help you work toward a solution to the problem.

5. Work with others to decide how you can bring attention to the global problem and its solutions.

GLOSSARY

atmosphere: the air that surrounds a planet

autism spectrum disorder: a disorder where someone may have difficulties in social interaction and communication, and in restricted or repetitive patterns of thought and behavior

carbon dioxide: a colorless, odorless gas that is naturally present in air, but which is also produced by burning fossil fuels, which contributes to climate change

carbon footprint: the amount of carbon dioxide (and other carbon compounds) a person or group releases into the atmosphere by burning fossil fuels

climate change: abnormal change in Earth's climate patterns caused by fossil fuels

emissions: something given off as a result of operating, such as carbon dioxide emissions from flying a plane

energy grid: a transmission system for electricity; power providers and consumers connected into one network by power lines

fossil fuel: a fuel (such as coal, oil, or natural gas) that is formed in the earth from the remains of living plants or animals; burning fossil fuels produces carbon dioxide and contributes to climate change

lawmaker: an elected government official who helps create laws that people must follow

parliament: a group of people responsible for making laws in certain kinds of governments, or the building where those people work

renewable energy: energy that comes from a source that cannot be used up or destroyed, such as wind or solar power

strike: when someone stops working or going to school in order to force someone else to agree to do something

summit: a meeting between the leaders of two or more governments

United Nations: an organization formed in 1945 so that its member countries could work together and cooperate better

US Congress: a group of lawmakers in the US government, made up of the Senate and the House of Representatives

viral: spread very quickly to many people, usually via the internet

READ MORE

Camerini, Valentina. *Greta's Story: The Schoolgirl Who Went on Strike to Save the Planet.* London: Simon and Schuster UK, 2019.

David, Alex. *Dying Off: Endangered Plants and Animals.* New York: Cavendish Square, 2020.

Herman, Gail. *What Is Climate Change?* New York: Penguin Workshop, 2018.

Iyer, Rani. *Endangered Energy: Investigating the Scarcity of Fossil Fuels.* North Mankato, MN: Capstone Press, 2014.

Thunberg, Greta. *No One Is Too Small to Make a Difference.* New York: Penguin, 2019.

INTERNET SITES

https://climatekids.nasa.gov/menu/play
Read more about alternative energy and play games with NASA Climate Kids.

https://youtu.be/qe_-LR8PpLk
Watch Greta address representatives from around the world at the UN Climate Summit.

https://www.youthclimatestrikeus.org
Find ways to get involved in combating climate change.

https://350.org/get-involved
Use the interactive map to find climate protests around the world.

INDEX